DORSET

TEASHOP

WALKS

By Robert Hesketh

www.roberthesketh.co.uk

Inspiring Places Publishing
2 Down Lodge Close
Alderholt
Fordingbridge
Hants.
SP6 3JA
www.inspiringplaces.co.uk
© Robert Hesketh 2018
All rights reserved
ISBN 978-0-9955964-2-9
Contains Ordnance Survey data © Crown copyright and database right (2011)

JURASSICCOAST
QUALITY
BUSINESS

Front cover: Clubmen's Down near Compton Abbas and inset - No 9 on the Green, Wimborne.
Rear cover: Shillingstone Station.
All photographs by the author except pages 5 (bottom), 13, 21, 24, 25, 27 (bottom), 30, 33 (inset), 39 (bottom) and 45 by Robert Westwood.

Introduction - *see back page for location and page numbers of walks.*

These circular walks have been selected to help you discover Dorset's wonderfully varied coast and countryside. They differ in length, but more importantly in terrain, so the time needed to complete will vary from one person to another. But why hurry? Each walk has its own character and there are many viewpoints and places of historical and geological interest en route. Please take them at your own pace and I'm sure you'll enjoy them as much as I have.

Every walk includes at least one teashop. Each is individual and several are really unusual, including one housed in a vintage railway carriage, one sited in a Victorian fort and another giving a grandstand view of an airfield. Menus vary, as do opening hours and days of business. It is advisable to phone in advance to check before setting out, or check their website.

Clothing and Footwear
Exploring Dorset on foot is a pleasure throughout the seasons – so long as you're prepared. Mud, puddles and some rough footing are par for the course, thus walking boots are ideal, but Wellingtons can't breathe or offer ankle support and sandals are inadequate.

The climate's (usually!) mild, but changeable. It's always wise to pack waterproofs and an extra warm layer in your rucksack. Gorse and nettles make trousers a better option than shorts, especially as they provide some protection from ticks, which may carry Lyme disease. If a tick does latch onto you, remove it carefully and promptly with tweezers.

Kit
Even in winter drinking water is essential – allow a litre on short walks, two on longer ones. Walking poles or a stick are a great bonus, ditto extra food and a mobile phone. Use the book's sketch maps as a general guide, but Ordnance Survey Explorer maps for detail. Explorers 116, 117, 118, 129 and Outdoor Leisure15 cover all the routes in this book.

The Countryside
Nothing beats walking for safe and healthy exercise, but please remember most cliff paths are unfenced and mind out for uneven and waterlogged ground. Please follow the Country Code; respect farmers' crops and leave gates closed or open as you find them and keep dogs under control, particularly during the lambing and bird nesting seasons.

Lyme Regis - Distance: 3 miles/4.8 km   Time: 2½ hours   Exertion: Easy
NB - Mileage indicators in all walk descriptions are intended as rough guides.

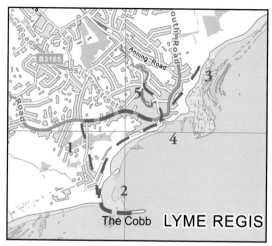

Start/parking: Holmbush car park, Pound Street, SY336920, DT7 3HX.
Terrain: Tarred paths and streets. One moderately long ascent and descent.
Stiles: 0
Public Toilets: At start and on seafront.
Maps: Explorer 116 or Landranger 193

Teashops

Lyme Regis has a great number and variety of teashops and cafés, both on the seafront and in the centre of town. Everything is made or baked on the premises at **Town Mill Bakery** (Coombe Street, 01297 444754). Meals are served all day, including afternoon teas with cakes, scones and jam. Recommended too is the **Courtyard Café** by the Town Mill (off Coombe Street, 01297 445757). The café uses flour from the Town Mill to bake bread, cakes, pastries and scones. Café and bakery both have outdoor and indoor seating.

As well as superb views of the Jurassic Coast, this short walk encompasses much of Lyme's handsome Georgian architecture and several places of geological and historical interest. The fully operational Town Mill and Lyme's great breakwater, the Cobb, are both en route, as are Lyme's Fossil Shop, Dinosaurland and the excellent Lyme Regis Museum. These all have fine fossil displays, testifying to the area's remarkable geology, especially its rich heritage of fossils, which helped to make it Britain's first natural World Heritage Site. Other points of interest include the Lifeboat station and the Aquarium.

1. Take the pedestrian exit on the eastern side of Holmbush car park. Walk down steps. Turn right into Cobb Lane. Turn left and down steps at the fingerpost signed "Seafront Gardens". Follow the winding paths downhill to the Lifeboat station and the Cobb. Explore both and the Aquarium, then

Lyme Regis from the Cobb.

return to the seafront.

2. 1 mile: Turn right along the seafront. Continue past Marine Parade and the clock tower. Follow the sea wall to its end.

3. 1¾ miles: Retrace your steps along the sea wall to the clock tower.

4. 2¼ miles: Turn right at the clock tower and right again in front of the Pilot Boat Inn. Turn left only 50m ahead (or divert right to visit Lyme Regis Museum) and walk up Coombe Street to the Town Mill Bakery. Continue ahead, and then turn left "Riverside Walk Town Mill". A group including an art gallery, brewery, pottery and Courtyard Café surrounds the Town Mill. After exploring these, retrace your steps to Coombe Street and divert left for a short distance to visit Dinosaurland Museum.

5. 2½ miles: Retrace your steps down Coombe Street to the Clock Tower. Either retrace your steps along the seafront to the car park or follow the main street (Broad Street) uphill. The Royal Lion Hotel takes pride of place among the many fine Georgian buildings, several with bow or bay windows. At the fork, continue left to the car park.

The Cobb

Lyme developed into a major port thanks to the Cobb protecting its otherwise exposed beach. It is not known exactly how old this man made harbour is, but it was storm damaged in 1313 and 1377 and rebuilt. During the 18th century, the Cobb was rebuilt, this time in mortared masonry. As Lyme was the only protected harbour along a dangerous stretch of coast, the government recognized its strategic importance at a time of threatened French invasion and footed the repair bill in 1792. The Cobb remains vital in protecting Lyme's coastal, fishing and leisure trades.

Lyme Regis Museum has an excellent marine fossil collection. Other exhibits range from fossil hunter extraordinaire Mary Anning to novelists Jane Austen and John Fowles, who used Lyme as a major setting in their writings. Maritime history and the Monmouth Rebellion also feature largely. www.lymeregismuseum.co.uk 01297 443370.

Dinosaurland Fossil Museum has over 8,000 specimens, many of them local. A time gallery explains the major geological periods and there is also a natural history room with a range of specimens. www.dinosaurland.co.uk 01297 443541.

Town Mill - Guided tours show how the restored Victorian milling machinery and the modern hydroelectric plant work. Each stage of the milling process is thoroughly explained. Contact 01297 444042 to check opening times and dates of milling days. www.townmill.org.uk

The Cobb.

The harbour from the Cobb.

West Bay - Distance: 5 miles/8 km Time: 2½ hours Exertion: Moderate

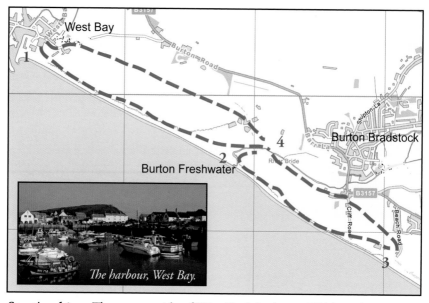

The harbour, West Bay.

Start/parking: The eastern side of West Bay's harbour, SY463904, DT6 4EN. Alternative parking nearby off Bridport Road.
Terrain: Coast Path and footpaths. One very steep ascent and descent.
Stiles: 8 **Public Toilets:** West Bay, Hive Beach.
Maps: Explorer OL15 or Landrangers 193 and 194

Teashops
Hive Beach Café (01308 897070) is beautifully situated and ideally placed half-way around the route. Open all day through the year, it also serves evening meals in summer. Cakes and biscuits are baked on the premises. Fresh fish and seafood is its speciality. Its sister cafés in Burton Bradstock and West Bay are both called **Watch House Café**. West Bay also offers the **Harbour Café**, the **Tea Station** (in the old railway station) and the **West Bay Tea Rooms**.

Starting from West Bay, with its pleasant medley of fishing boats and leisure craft, this walk includes magnificent view of the Jurassic Coast and a pleasing inland return. We begin at the harbour, which dates from the 1740s, when a channel was cut through the beach and a hollow excavated behind it.

1. The harbour divides West Bay's two beaches. Walk onto East Beach by the

Bridport Arms Hotel. Turn left (east) onto the Coast Path. The sharp climb up East Cliff is rewarded with magnificent views. Continue along the clifftop path.

2. 1¼ miles: Reaching the far end of Burton Freshwater, turn left and walk ahead parallel to the River Bride for 500m. Cross the footbridge. Follow the Coast Path for "Burton Bradstock" to the Hive Beach Café.

3. 2¾ miles: Retrace your steps from the café for 300m to a path junction. Bear right, signed "Burton Bradstock". Arriving in the village, turn right and almost immediately left into Southover. Continue ahead at the end of this lane signed "Coast Path Freshwater".

4. 3½ miles: At the next path junction turn right "West Bay". Recross the footbridge you crossed earlier and start retracing your steps "Coast Path West Bay". At the next path junction either retrace your steps along the Coast Path or turn right onto the signed "Footpath". (This inland route via the caravan park and golf course is pleasant, but does not compare with the Coast Path for views). Continue through the caravan park, past Reception and uphill past a further street of mobile homes. When the lane curves right, turn left. Go through a metal gate and turn right as signed. Follow the signed footpath through the golf course. Beware flying golf balls and do not deviate from the signed path. Exit the golf course via a stile and follow the path downhill to a lane. Turn left and follow the lane to the harbour.

West Bay and the Watch House Café (arrowed).

Abbotsbury - Distance: 4 miles/6.4 km or 2¾ miles/4.4 km
Time: 2 hours or 1½ hours Exertion: Easy

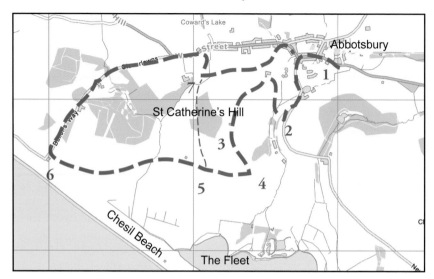

Start/parking: Abbotsbury car park, signed at eastern edge of village, SY579853, DT3 4JL.
Terrain: Footpaths and pavement. One moderate ascent, one steeper descent.
Stiles: 2
Public Toilets: Back Street, Abbotsbury and Chesil Bank car park.
Maps: Explorer OL15 or Landranger 194

Abbotsbury is an exceptionally attractive stone built village with a long history. This walk includes Abbotsbury's key historic sites and great views. Abbotsbury grew around the eleventh century abbey. Although this was largely destroyed during the Dissolution (1536-40), there are substantial ruins along Church Street, where some of the beautiful masonry has been re-used in other buildings. The abbey's Tithe Barn is its most impressive survival. One of the largest in England at 272ft (83m) long, it dates from around 1400. Along with its ancient pond, it is now a children's farm.

Also en route is St Catherine's Chapel. It was probably built as a pilgrim chapel at about the same time as the Tithe Barn. Perched boldly on its hill, it survived the Dissolution because it was a valuable seamark. The longer version of the route includes two optional extras: a visit to Chesil Beach and Abbotsbury's sub-tropical gardens. Internationally famed for its camellias and magnolias, the garden is also noted for its rhododendrons and hydrangeas. Another visit which may be added is Abbotsbury Swannery (admission charge). This has up to 600 birds and is the oldest managed swan population in the world, first recorded in 1393.

1. Turn left out of the car park into Rodden Row, with its medley of 18th and 19th century listed cottages. Turn left again into Church Street. St Nicholas's has a stone effigy of an abbot in the porch; a 1638 chancel ceiling with beautiful plasterwork; gilded reredos and a fine brass chandelier. Continue down Church Street past Abbey House, with its tearooms. This stands on the site of the old monastic infirmary and incorporates stone from the Abbey. Continue to the Tithe Barn. Branch right along the lane (Grove Lane) signed "Swannery Pedestrians" and continue past houses.

2. ½ mile: Turn right over a stone stile "Coast Path Chesil Beach". Follow the path right. Keep right "Abbotsbury St Catherine's Chapel". Reaching a gate, turn sharp left "St Catherine's Chapel". Looking back are splendid views of Abbotsbury, especially on a summer's evening when long shadows pick out the details and define the strip lynchets (medieval cultivation terraces) on the slope. Other examples of strip lynchets can be seen on the Worth Matravers walk, page 22.

3. 1 mile: Take the path on the Chapel's south-east side "Coast Path and Swannery". Head downhill over the turf, aiming for the southern edge of Chapel Coppice. Pick up a steep path downhill at the edge of the coppice. Follow this down to a marker stone near the foot of the hill.

4. 1¼ miles: Turn right "Sub-Tropical Gardens" along a well-worn path. On your left are Chesil Bank and Abbotsbury Swannery. Continue past a World War Two pillbox and through a gate, signed "Coast Path".

The Fleet.

5. 1¾ miles: Reaching a path junction either turn left "Chesil Beach" for the full route or turn right "Abbotsbury" to reduce the walk by 1¼ miles. If you take the short cut, simply rejoin the directions at Point 7. For the full route, follow the Coast Path behind Chesil Beach and turn right into the car park or divert left onto the path over the shingle bank to visit the beach.

6. 2½ miles: Turn right out of the car park and follow the lane uphill past the sub-tropical gardens. Join the field edge path parallel to the right side of the lane. Reaching the road, cross carefully. Turn right along the pavement for only 100m. Recross the road and walk ahead on the track "Chesil Beach".

7. 3¼ miles: Turn left at the path junction 300m ahead, signed "Village Chapel Hill" (NB Bear right if you took the short cut and follow the directions from here). Take the second track on your left "Abbotsbury Village". Turn right onto the main street. The Old Schoolhouse Tearooms are on your left, Bellenie's Bakehouse and the Ilchester Arms on your right. Continue down the street past the Abbotsbury Tearooms. Follow left into Rodden Row for the car park.

Abbotsbury from Chapel Hill.

Teashops

The **Old Schoolhouse Tearooms** (01305 871808) in Back Street offers a varied menu including homemade scones, cakes, quiches and soups, with apple cake and homity pies as specialities. The flower filled courtyard garden is warm and sunny. Other options include the **Abbey House Tearooms**, **Abbotsbury Tearooms**, **Bellenie's Bakehouse**, the beach café at Chesil Bank car park, plus tea or coffee at the Ilchester Arms.

Beaminster - Distance: 6¾ miles/10.8 km Time: 3½ hours Exertion: Moderate

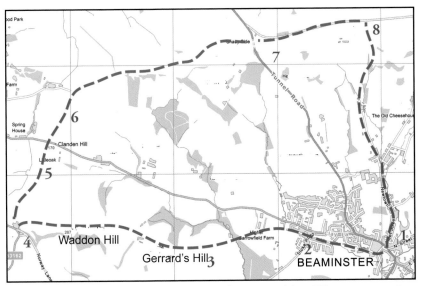

Start/parking: Yarn Barton car park, ST481013, DT8 3EF.
Terrain: Footpaths, bridleways, quiet lanes and roads. Parts may be muddy. One long ascent and descent.
Stiles: 8
Public Toilets: Beaminster
Maps: Explorer 116 or Landranger 193

This exploration offers memorable views and a deal of historic interest - and yet you're likely to have much of the route to yourself in this little known corner of West Dorset. Beaminster is an intriguing town, with a delightful mix of buildings in local stone from several eras in its triangular square and neighbouring streets. A splendid 15th century church, St Mary's, has many interesting features. These include the dignified west tower; the original Norman font and the Strode monuments. En route we pass the outer ramparts of Waddon Hill Roman fort, whilst Gerrard's Hill (574ft/174m) offers a panorama of West Dorset, a vast swathe of rolling hills and patchwork fields stretching to the sea. Towards the end of the walk further fine views open out, northwards into Somerset and south over Beaminster.

1. Turn left out of the car park into the Square with its 1906 memorial standing on the site of the market cross. Follow the sign for St Mary's Church down Church Street. Continue down Church Street into Shorts Lane and

onto the bridleway and footpath.

2. ¾ mile: Reaching a lane, turn left, then almost immediately right into Half Acre Lane. After 100m, turn left into the signed footpath. Cross the field ahead diagonally. Continue ahead signed "Chart Knolle". The path drops into a copse. Ignore footpaths right and left. Continue ahead "Chart Knolle" and uphill over stiles to the beech clump and triangulation point on Gerrard's Hill.

3. 1½ miles: Follow the signed path downhill to Chart Knolle. At the next path junction continue ahead for "Stoke Knapp". The humps and bumps in

Beaminster.

the ground on your left as you approach Stoke Knapp are part of Waddon Hill Roman Fort.

4. 2¾ miles: Turn right at Stoke Knapp, signed "Broadwindsor". Follow the signed path across fields. Cut diagonally right across the last field to a road.

5. 3¼ miles: Cross carefully and follow the track ahead.

6. 3½ miles: Reaching a broad track (Common Water Lane), turn right. Please keep to the track to protect the spring flowers.

7. 5 miles: Continue ahead when Common Water Lane meets a tarred road. Although marked as a B road this attracts little traffic.

8. 5½ miles: Turn right onto footpath signed "Beaminster". Follow this downhill, across fields and into a lane. Continue ahead to the start.

Teashops

Beaminster offers several choices, including the **Art Deco Café**, **Bridge House Brasserie** and **Vicki's Sandwich Bar**. **Cilla and Camilla's Café** (01308 863477) is conveniently situated in the Square and has a courtyard garden. Teas, coffees, soft drinks and light meals are offered through the day. Apple cake is a speciality, whilst scones come from the nearby bakery.

Cerne Abbas - Distance: 2½ miles/4 km Time: 2 hours Exertion: Easy

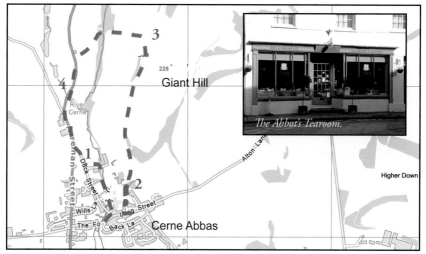

The Abbot's Tearoom.

Start/parking: Signed car park near Giant Viewpoint, opposite village hall. (Note, not the one by the viewpoint.) ST663014, DT2 7AL.
Terrain: Mainly footpaths, short sections of pavement.
Stiles: 1
Public Toilets: Cerne Abbas
Maps: Explorer 117 or Landranger 194

Cerne Abbas has a remarkable collection of historic buildings in brick, stone and timber. Its abbey, tithe barn and church are all included on this route, as well as its historic inns and the Silver Well.

After exploring part of the beautiful Cerne Valley, our walk concludes with the remarkable Cerne Abbas Giant. Cut into the chalk hillside, the Giant is 180ft long, 167ft wide and brandishes a club 120ft long in his right hand. Despite his size, he could not have survived without regular attention to keep back encroaching weeds.

An unmistakably triumphant and phallic symbol, the Giant's age and origins have been much debated. Although the earliest record of his existence only dates from 1742, the Giant is most probably Romano-British in origin. He is thought to be a British Hercules, a cult figure symbolizing strength and fertility. Certainly, he resembles Roman coins, statuettes and Castor ware representing Hercules. He may well date from the time of Commodus (AD180-93). After defeating the Scots in 187, Commodus declared himself Hercules incarnate and added Hercules Romanus to his titles.

Cerne Valley from Giant Hill.

It is impossible to be sure whether the Giant we see today is the true original or one modified (or possibly designed) by later and maybe ruder hands; especially as other British chalk cut figures, including the Wilmington Long Man in Sussex and the Uffington White Horse in Oxfordshire, show some change of form and character over the centuries. For many, the enigmas surrounding the Giant add to his appeal.

1. Turn left out of the car park and right for "Village Centre" along the riverside path. Keep ahead at the path junction and continue past the garden entrance to the Abbot's Tearooms. Turn left to the main village street, then turn almost immediately right along it. Follow the street past the telephone booth. Take the first footpath left signed "Barton Meadows Farm". Do not enter the private drive, but the Tithe Barn may be viewed from the footpath 50m ahead. Built in the 14th century, the Tithe Barn was converted to a private dwelling in the 18th century. Retrace your steps to Abbot's Tearooms. Opposite is the New Inn, a late 17th/18th century coaching inn. Continue along the main street (Long Street) to the Royal Oak. This delightful thatched building has an early 16th century core with 18th and 19th century alterations. Features include period photographs, exposed beams, flagstones and an open fire. Turn left to visit the church. Originally built by the monks about 1300, it has medieval wall paintings, a splendid Jacobean pulpit and a 15th century stone screen. Continue along Abbey Street. Cerne Abbey is a private house incorporating parts of the medieval monastic gatehouse, but largely rebuilt from the 18th century. Go through the gate (admission charge) to see the Abbey Guest House and the Abbot's porch with its lovely oriel windows. Retrace your steps to the entrance.

2. 1 mile: From the entrance to Cerne Abbey, turn through a stone arch. The footpath immediately divides. Walk ahead only 50m to visit the Silver Well, with its sculpted stone seat representing the Bible's Living Waters. Retrace your steps to the footpath sign and turn right to exit the graveyard. The path divides again. Keep ahead. Cross a stile and keep left on the lower path. (NB do not climb the steps). Stay on the lower path as you walk under Giant Hill. Several informal footpaths have been worn into the steep hillside, more than are shown on the Explorer map. After ¾ mile bear left through a small gate.

3. 1¾ miles: Walk ahead as signed, keeping the hedge on your right. Continue ahead through trees and over a footbridge as signed. Follow the path uphill through trees. Cut diagonally left across the field ahead as signed, aiming just left of the house. Bear left and stay on the footpath, which follows the field edge parallel to the road. At the far end of the field, turn right and cross the road carefully.

4. 2¼ miles: Follow the road left for only 30m. Bear right onto a signed footpath. Follow this left along the field edge to a lane. Bear left along the lane and then right along the road. Keep to the edge and join the verge. Cross the road to the Giant Viewing Area. Follow the lane ahead (note the early 19th century milestone on your right). Turn left into the car park.

The Cerne Giant.

The Abbot's Porch.

Teashops
The Abbot's Tearoom (01300 341349) has a pleasant, sunny garden. Open daily for breakfasts, lunches and teas, it offers homemade cakes and biscuits. Note, it is open all year except for January, but closed winter Mondays.

Weymouth and Nothe Fort - Distance: 3¼ miles/5.2 km Time: 2 hours
Exertion: Easy

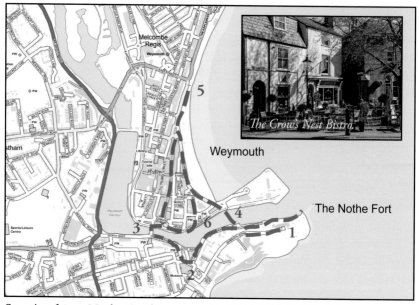

The Crows Nest Bistro

Weymouth

The Nothe Fort

Start/parking: Nothe Gardens car park, SY684787, DT4 8UF.
Terrain: Footpaths, pavements and pedestrianised street. Two flights of
steps – alternative ramps.
Stiles: 0
Public Toilets: Nothe Gardens and Seafront.
Maps: Explorer OL15 or Landranger 194

Although this walk might be completed in two hours, there is so much of
interest that a full day is warranted to appreciate Weymouth's rich architectural
heritage, the changing life on its busy quays and to explore its historic sites.
These include Nothe's Victorian fort; Weymouth Museum and Tudor House.

1. Walk through Nothe Gardens, but divert right for a superb view of Portland
Harbour. After visiting Nothe Fort, exit by the main entrance and turn
immediately right down either ramp or steps. Turn right again and continue
along the pier for superb views of Nothe Fort and Weymouth's handsome
seafront. Start retracing your steps. Continue along the quay, past attractive
bow windowed terrace houses. Branch left up Hope Street to Hope Square,
where there is a choice of cafés, including the Crow's Nest Bistro. At the
time of writing (2017), Brewer's Quay in Hope Square was scheduled for
redevelopment, a mix of apartments, shops and cafés. It houses Weymouth

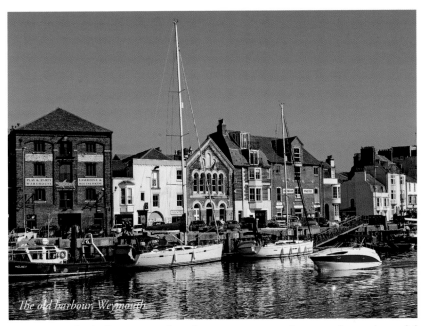

The old harbour, Weymouth

Museum, which features archaeology, paintings, photographs and model ships.

2. 1mile: From Hope Square, bear right signed "Tudor House". Turn right into Trinity Street. Tudor House is an early 17th century furnished house (01305 779711 for opening times). Opposite are the Old Rooms, also four centuries old. Return to the Quay and bear left along Trinity Road. Number 2 bears a plaque to former owner, Ralph Allen (1693-1764) "whose patronage first established Weymouth as a resort." Allen was Mayor of Bath and played a leading role in its development as a fashionable spa, using Bath stone from his own quarries. Through him, Bath stone was also employed in Weymouth. Continue past more handsome Georgian houses to the 16th century King's Arms, with its fine 18th century facade.

3. 1¼ miles: Turn right over the bascule bridge and right again onto the quay. Reaching the Ship Inn, divert left for 50m. The 17th century building on your left has a cannon ball embedded in the masonry – probably a souvenir of the Civil War. Return to the quay and continue past the Custom House, which served H.M. Customs from the early 19th century until 1985.

4. 1¾ miles: Reaching the funfair, turn left onto the Esplanade and follow it to King George III's statue (1810) and his bathing machine. George popularised Weymouth and set the fashion for sea bathing and seaside holidays. Continue past the war memorial to the Clock Tower, erected in 1887 to celebrate Queen Victoria's Golden Jubilee.

5. 2¼ miles: Retrace your steps. Using the crossing just behind King George's statue, bear around left into pedestrianised St Mary Street. The 16th century Black Dog was originally The Dove, but renamed after Weymouth started trading with the newly founded colonies of Newfoundland and Labrador, at which time the landlord acquired a black Newfoundland dog. A plaque relates the pub's smuggling connections and the grisly murder recorded here in 1758.

6. 2¾ miles: Reaching the Custom House Quay you have the choice of re-crossing by the bridge or the rowboat ferry (operates April to September, weather permitting). Either turn left and walk down the Quay to the ferry to enjoy a different perspective of the harbour, or re-cross the bascule bridge and retrace your steps along Trinity Road and the Quay. Whichever option you choose, continue until you reach the first flight of steps (or the ramp) and return to the start.

Nothe Fort

Nothe headland guards the entrance to Weymouth Harbour. Guns were sited on Nothe Fort from the mid-16th century and a small fort was added during the Civil War. The much larger Palmerston fort we see today was begun in 1860. Built of large blocks of Portland stone, granite and brick and supported by heavy earth banks to absorb shock, it was completed in 1872.

Exploring the fort reveals several features inherited from medieval castles, such as the barbican and dry moat, but also the rapid development of artillery from muzzle loading to breech loading guns. On display too are anti-aircraft guns from Nothe's Second World War service. www.nothefort.org.uk 01305 766626

Teashops

There is a huge choice of teashops and cafés en route, including the **Fort View Café** (01305 766626) in Nothe Fort, offering breakfast, light lunches and cream teas. The **Crow's Nest Bistro** in Hope Square (Point 2, 01305 786930) has indoor and outdoor seating and is open from 9 to 5, plus summer evenings. Phone or check website for full opening times. The varied menu includes cream teas and cakes, as well as seafood and tapas.

Portland, Church Ope Cove and Easton - Distance: 4½ miles/7.2 km
Time: 2½ hours   Exertion: Moderate

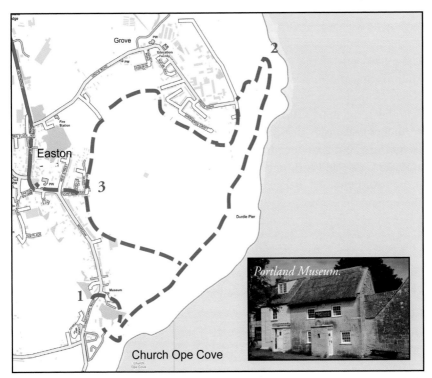

Church Ope Cove

Portland Museum.

Start/parking: Signed car park "Church Ope Cove/Portland Museum", SY695712, DT5 1HS.

Terrain: Coastpath, footpaths, pavement. Two steep ascents, one steep descent.

Stiles: 1

Public Toilets: Easton Square

Maps: Explorer OL15 or Landranger 194

As well as fine coastal views, this circuit includes much of historic interest, including a castle, a ruined church and Portland's excellent museum. There is also a section of disused railway and a ruined church – Portland's oldest surviving building.

Portland Museum (seasonal opening, 01305 821804) was donated by Dr Marie Stopes. Her former cottage contains agricultural exhibits, domestic artefacts and a maritime room packed with items from shipwrecks. A second cottage (Avice's) contains quarrymen's tools and sculptures and some excellent fossils.

Nearby is Rufus Castle. The original Norman castle was rebuilt in 1258. In its turn, this 13th century castle provided the foundations for the solid stone keep or blockhouse we see today. This was built in the mid-15th century by Richard, Duke of York. (*Note: the castle is on private land).

1. Turn left out of the car park. Turn right "Museum and Church Ope". After visiting the museum, follow the Public Footpath past Rufus Castle. Either continue ahead "Coast Path" (shortening the route by 500m) or divert right down the steps. Turn right again "13th century church ruins". This is St Andrew's, the isle's first parish church. It stands on a site occupied since Saxon times, but abandoned in 1753 following landslips. Retrace your steps to Rufus Castle and turn right "Coast Path". Continue ahead "East Weares" at the path junction. Below, on your right, look out for quarrymen's stone huts among the extensive abandoned workings.

2. 1½ miles: Turn left as signed "Coast Path". Leaving the level course of the former Portland Branch Railway, the path climbs steeply in a zig zag to the top of the cliff. The flint banding in the limestone is very obvious, showing successive layers of deposition. Reaching the top of the cliff, turn left along the lane under the outer walls of the grim prison. Continue ahead

Church Ope Cove

through the visitors' car park. Turn right and follow "Permissive Path" signs around houses. Turn right again "Public Footpath". Follow this past houses. Continue through a metal gate. Reaching a path junction, turn left. The path becomes a track. Stay on the track and ignore diversions. Cross a lane and continue ahead as signed through a play park. When the path divides, walk ahead to a lane.

3. 3 miles: Divert right for the Easton cafés (or follow the directions from the paragraph below and shorten the walk by ¾ mile). Reaching Wakeham (the main street), turn right and follow the pavement round to Easton Square. Turn left opposite the Co-Op for the Sugar Loaf Café or continue ahead 50m to Whitestone's Café. Retrace your steps to Point 3. Turn right "Public Footpath". Reaching a disused quarry, turn left and follow the quarry track to "Coast Path Church Ope Cove". Follow the path back to the museum and car park.

Teashops

Easton has two teashops. The **Sugar Loaf Café** offers a traditional, home cooked menu from breakfast, through lunch to tea (01305 821997). **Whitestone's Café** (01305 561597) is licensed and also offers a menu based on local produce through the day, plus a sculpture garden and art gallery to enjoy. Additionally, there is **Hayloft Café** (01305 821286, limited seasonal opening) in Pennsylvania Castle opposite the car park. Licensed, this offers fresh fruit, vegetables and salads from the estate. **Portland Museum** (01305 821804) also sells tea and coffee, plus books and guides.

Alternatively, there are two cafés nearby both with great views out to sea. For a unique experience try the **Jailhouse Café** at the Verne Prison (DT5 1EQ, 01305 825186), staffed by risk assessed inmates. At Portland Bill, **The Lobster Pot** (DT5 2JT, 01305 820242) is in a fabulous position with lots of seating outside, perfect for a sunny day.

The Lobster Pot at Portland Bill (arrowed).

Worth Matravers - Distance: 5½ miles/8.8 km Time: 3 hours Exertion: Challenging

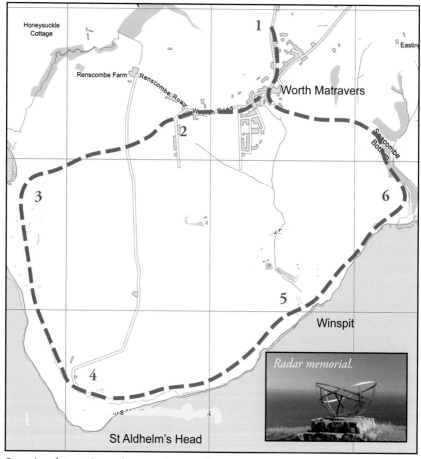

Radar memorial.

Start/parking: Signed car park, Worth Matravers SY974777, BH19 3LE.
Terrain: Coast Path, footpaths, short section of quiet lane. One tough ascent and descent (relieved by steps) and several lesser slopes.
Stiles: 6
Public Toilets: At start.
Maps: Explorer OL15 or Landranger 195

This route includes some of the finest cliff top walking in Dorset and splendid views east from Winspit and west from St Aldhelm's Head, with its Coastwatch station, medieval chapel and memorial to the crucial pioneering radar research carried out here during 1940-42. Alas, there was no Coastwatch or radar in

1786 to warn the East Indiaman Halsewell or raise the alarm when she was wrecked in a storm under Seacombe Cliffs. Although 82 passengers and crew were rescued by local people after two sailors managed to scale the cliffs and alert rescuers, 160 died. Among the dead was Captain Pearce, who refused to abandon his two daughters.

Allow extra time for a small diversion from point 5 to Winspit's historic quarry caves, where the roofs are supported by columns of rock. During the 18th and early 19th centuries smuggling was rife all along the Dorset coast and quarry caves such as these made good storage places for smuggled goods, whilst quarrymen supplied a ready labour force. Winches used for lowering stone onto barges could readily haul contraband up from waiting luggers.

Worth Matravers is a handsome village of Purbeck stone. The steep hillsides around are deeply marked by strip lynchets.

1. Turn right out of the car park. Walk past the Square and Compass and turn right. Follow the lane past the village pond, the Tea and Supper Room and the church to Weston Farm.

2. ½ mile: Take the concrete track, signed "St Aldhelm's Head". After only 50m, turn right through a gate. Follow the field path to the car park. Exit the car park via a kissing gate and follow the well-beaten path diagonally across a field.

3. 1mile: Cross a stile and turn left onto the Coast Path. Continue to St Aldhelm's Chapel and the Coastwatch station.

4. 2¼ miles: Continue east on the Coast Path.

5. 3¾ miles: Arriving at a path junction near Winspit, turn right "Seacombe". Only 50m ahead, the path divides. To explore Winspit Quarries, divert right.

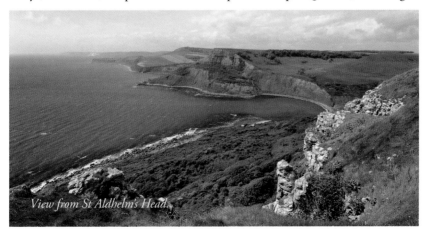

View from St Aldhelm's Head.

Otherwise, turn left and follow the Coast Path as it curves left, then turns right to climb East Man via steps. (Ignore any side turnings). Both East Man and West Man have prominent strip lynchets.

6. 4½ miles: Reaching Seacombe Bottom, turn left "Worth". When the path divides, keep left "Worth". Arriving in Worth Matravers, turn right and retrace your steps to the car park.

The Tea and Supper Room.

Teashops
The Tea and Supper Room offers lunches, teas and evening meals with indoor and courtyard garden seating. The varied menu includes several speciality teas, coffee, chocolate, fruit juice and alcoholic beverages, plus cream teas. Light lunches and up to three course evening meals are also offered. It is normally open Wednesday to Saturday in season, with limited winter opening. (01929 439368).

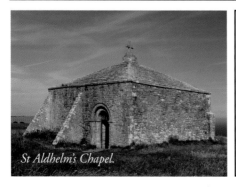
St Aldhelm's Chapel.

St Aldhelm's Chapel
First recorded in the 13th century, St Aldhelm's is dedicated to Aldhelm, the first Bishop of Sherborne, who lived in the 7th century. Its square plan with the angles pointing to the cardinal points of the compass are most unusual for a church building.

Langton Matravers - Distance: 7 miles/11.2 km Time: 3½ hours
Exertion: Moderate

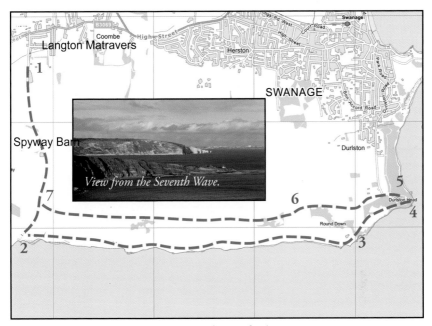

View from the Seventh Wave.

Start/parking: Car park at the end of Durnford Drove SY997783, nearest
postcode BH19 3HG (follow signs for Langton House).
Terrain: Coastpath and footpaths. Some ascents and descents, but nothing
arduous.
Stiles: 9
Public Toilets: Durlston Head
Maps: Explorer OL15 or Landranger 195
Durlston Castle: 01929 424443 durlston.co.uk

As well as superb views of the Purbeck coast; Old Harry Rocks; Poole Bay and
the Needles, this walk offers excellent bird and dolphin watching opportunities
from Durlston Head. Much of the walk passes through carefully managed
hay meadows, which support a wealth of wildflowers, butterflies and moths.
Among several old quarries en route is Dancing Ledge, from where blocks
of Portland stone where winched down to waiting barges. This secluded
landing place was exploited by smugglers, who used the quarry caves and
nearby Spyway Barn to store contraband. Smugglers also used Tilly Whim
quarry caves near Durlston Head. In the 1790s the church roof at Langton
Matravers collapsed under the weight of 200 brandy barrels stored there. One
worshipper was killed and several injured.

Durlston Castle was built in 1887 by George Burt, who made his fortune in Purbeck stone. This remarkable Victorian building has audio visual presentations of Purbeck's geology and wildlife, plus an art gallery, a shop selling books and souvenirs and a café/restaurant. En route, we pass the Great Globe, a 40 ton limestone sphere representing the Earth.

1. Follow the stony track south from the car park. At the junction, continue ahead "Dancing Ledge" onto a grassy track, past Spyway Barn and across fields. When the main track descends steps, divert slightly right to avoid loose footing.
2. 1 mile: Turn left (east) onto the Coast Path, or divert over a stile to Dancing Ledge.

Thrift on the Purbeck coast.

3. 3¼ miles: Continue east past the lighthouse on Anvil Point and Tilly Whim caves.
4. 3¾ miles: Follow the Coast Path past the limestone globe and round Durlston Head to Durlston Castle.
5. 4¼ miles: Take the path signed "Woodland Wildlife and Victorian Trails". Continue ahead at a path junction. Turn left onto a tarmac drive. Ignore turnings on your right. Continue ahead on a clear path parallel to the Coast Path, passing through a gate and later crossing a small footbridge.
6. 5 miles: When the path divides, continue ahead on the signed "Upper Path" parallel to the sea. It divides a second time. Continue ahead, following the ridge and the direction arrows – some of which were obscured by vegetation at

the time of writing. The path continues ahead with the wall on your right to a small gate. Continue ahead across access land (not marked on the Explorer map as a footpath) and over stiles to meet the path to Spyway Barn.

7. 6¼ miles: Turn right and retrace your steps via Spyway Barn to the start.

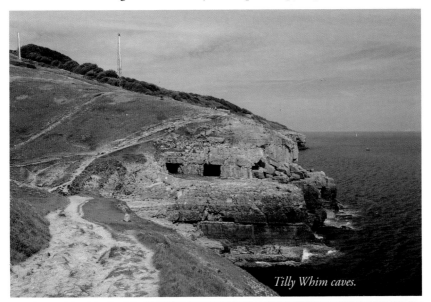

Tilly Whim caves.

Durlston Castle.

Teashop

Durlston Castle's **Seventh Wave** café/restaurant (01929 421111) offers high teas, cream teas, toasted teacakes, Dorset apple cake and Purbeck ice cream. Also on the extensive menu are light meals and salads; full cooked meals; sandwiches and paninis; plus teas and coffees and a licensed bar. Open all year. The coastal views to Old Harry Rocks are excellent.

Corfe Castle - Distance: 5 miles/8 km Time: 2½ hours Exertion: Moderate

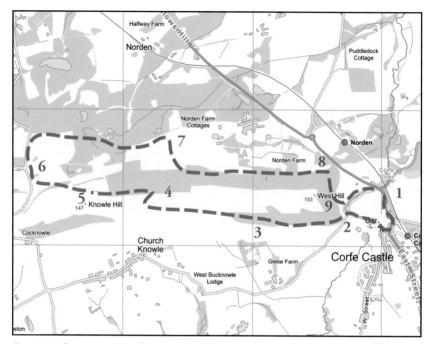

Start/parking: National Trust's Corfe Castle car park SY959825, BH20 5EZ.

Terrain: Footpaths, one short lane section. One steep ascent and descent.

Stiles: 4

Public Toilets: At start.

Maps: Explorer OL15 or Landranger 195

1. Cross the road and take the "Purbeck Way" footpath ahead. This leads past the ruins of West Mill. Continue ahead at the first signpost. At the second signpost, divert left "The Rings". Cross the lane carefully and divert immediately right to the Rings.

2. ½ mile: Retrace your steps across the lane. Go through the kissing gate in front of you and turn left onto the well-beaten path. Continue ahead "Cocknowle" at the next waymark.

3. 1 mile: When the path divides, keep left "Underhill Path". Continue past a lime kiln. At the next path junction, turn sharp right opposite a water trough and follow the track steeply uphill to meet the ridge path.

4. 1¾ miles: Turn left along the ridge path, keeping the fence on your right.

5. 2 miles: At the memorial stone, turn right "East Creech". Cross the

stile ahead and follow the path steeply downhill to a lane. Here, there is a memorial to the Creech Barrow Seven, one of the secret guerrilla units formed in 1940 to undermine any German occupation of Britain.

6. 2¼ miles: Turn right along the lane for 400m. Turn right onto the bridlepath "Norden Farm Corfe". Ignore side turnings and stick to the main woodland track. When the track divides, turn right over a footbridge for "Norden Farm".

7. 3¼ miles: Turn right through a kissing gate and follow the signed footpath along the edge of the campsite and through two more gates. Turn left along the woodland path.

8. 4 miles: Pass through a gate and follow the path right, around the foot of Knowle Hill.

9. 4¼ miles: Reaching a path junction, turn left "Corfe Castle" and right 50m ahead. Follow the footpath to Corfe Castle Tearooms. Turn left to visit the castle itself and to access the footpath to the car park. To do this, cross the bridge and turn right by the Barbican.

Corfe Castle from the Rings.

Corfe Castle

Standing on a steep 180ft (55m) high hill, Corfe Castle commands a gap in the chalk ridge, the natural gateway to Purbeck. This circuit offers views of Corfe's famous castle from all angles, including that seen by King Stephen's forces from their siege castle, The Rings, which they built in 1138/39. However, Corfe Castle and its massive 69ft (21m) high stone keep proved too tough a nut to crack and Stephen abandoned his two sieges.

Over 500 years later, when the castle had been further extended and fortified, the Rings were re-used as a base for guns during the Civil War by Parliamentarians besieging the castle. Although Lady Mary Bankes's 80 defenders were outnumbered by 500-600 Parliamentarians, they held out for six weeks until relieved by Royalist troops. Lady Mary held the castle successfully during a second siege in 1645, until one of her own officers treacherously admitted enemy soldiers.

She was awarded the seals and keys of Corfe Castle for her bravery, but the castle was "slighted" by Parliamentarian sappers. Despite using large quantities of explosives, it took several months to render the massive castle indefensible. Nonetheless, it remains a powerful and romantic monument to England's medieval castle builders.

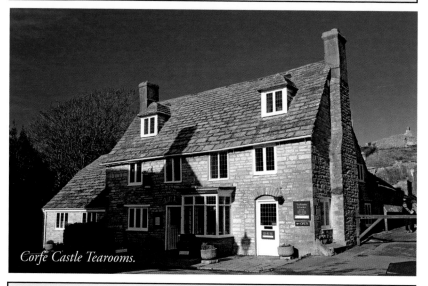

Corfe Castle Tearooms.

Teashops

The National Trust's 18th century **Corfe Castle Tearooms** (01929 481332) are open all year and have seating inside and outside in an attractive garden with an excellent view of the castle. The menu includes lunches, cream teas, soup and sandwiches, as well as tea, coffee, fruit juices and cider. The scones and cakes are all homemade.

Alternatively, there are the National Trust Tearooms at the car park and also the **Model Village Tearooms** on the opposite side of Corfe's Square. This has courtyard tables and indoor seating too. Scones and cakes are home baked. Licensed, it offers breakfasts, light lunches and cream teas.

Studland and Old Harry Rocks - Distance: 6¼ miles/10 km Time: 3½ hours Exertion: Moderate

Middle Beach, Studland.

Start/parking: Knoll Beach car park (National Trust) SZ033885, BH19 3AH.
Terrain: Coastpath, track, quiet lanes. One steady ascent; one sharper descent. Beware unfenced cliffs.
Stiles: 0
Public Toilets: Knoll Beach, Middle Beach and South Beach.
Maps: Explorer OL15 or Landranger 195

As well as stunning views of Old Harry Rocks, Studland Bay and Swanage Bay, this attractive coastal route has much of interest. Studland Bay was used as a D Day training area in 1943/44. En route we pass large pointed concrete blocks known as "Dragon's Teeth", installed as anti-tank defences. Fort Henry observation bunker was built by Canadian engineers and named after Fort Henry, Ontario. Churchill, Eisenhower and King George VI used it to watch D Day training in the bay. We also pass the Bankes Arms – a control base during WW2 - and a diversion along South Beach leads to a WW2 pillbox.

Handfast Point and Old Harry Rocks represent the eastern end of the fossil rich Jurassic Coast, which stretches 95 miles west to Exmouth in Devon and includes rocks covering 185 million years of the Earth's history. The massive chalk cliffs were deposited in a shallow, tropical sea around 65 million years ago at the end of the Cretaceous Period. Following this came the great extinction when the dinosaurs, ammonites and many other species were wiped out, probably due to the impact of a giant asteroid.

1. Follow the Coast Path south from Knoll Beach car park and beach café – or walk along the beach if the tide is low. Look out for the "Dragon's Teeth", found behind the Middle Beach huts (at SZ036830).
2. ½ mile: Follow the Coast Path past the café. Turn right up the tarred track as signed and left by Groom's Cottages. Passing Fort Henry, the Coast Path turns right up to a lane.
3. 1mile: Turn left past the Bankes Arms. Divert left to see South Beach, or to visit Joe's Café. At the far end of the beach is a WW2 concrete pillbox. Retrace your steps to the lane. Turn left and left again, joining the public bridleway to Handfast Point, which offers classic views of Old Harry Rocks and the Pinnacles.
4. 2½ miles: Follow the Coast Path south towards Ballard Point. When the path divides, keep left on the Coast Path as it curves around Ballard Point

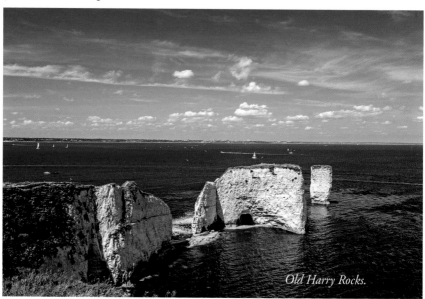

Old Harry Rocks.

and reveals a splendid view of Swanage Bay. Divert right through a gate to the concrete triangulation pillar. Follow the Purbeck Way along the ridge. Continue through a gate, past a boundary marker "Studland Manor 1776".

5. 4½ miles: Reaching a path junction and fingerpost, turn sharp right "Studland". Continue past houses and along the tarred lane to Manor Farm Tearooms.

6. 5¼ miles: Either divert left to visit Studland church, a rare survival of Norman architecture, or turn right "The Beach". Follow the lane as it curves left past the Bankes Arms. Retrace your steps via Fort Henry and Middle Beach to the car park.

Teashops

There are teashops at Knoll Beach, Middle Beach, South Beach and Manor Farm towards the end of the walk. All offer indoor and outdoor seating. **Knoll Beach Café** (01929 450259) is the largest. Open all year for breakfasts, main meals and cream teas, it offers the largest menu and is licensed. **Middle Beach Café** is also licensed and has a varied menu. At the time of writing (2017) plans to demolish the café and rebuild it were being mooted – and a petition was going to keep it.

Joe's Café on South Beach offers good value for money, with light snacks, including homemade brownies and flapjacks. Housed in converted farm buildings, **Manor Farm Tearooms** is decorated with local period photographs. The menu includes light lunches, homemade cakes and cream teas.

Studland Bay and inset, the café at Knoll Beach.

Wareham - Distance: 5 miles/8 km Time: 2½ hours Exertion: Easy

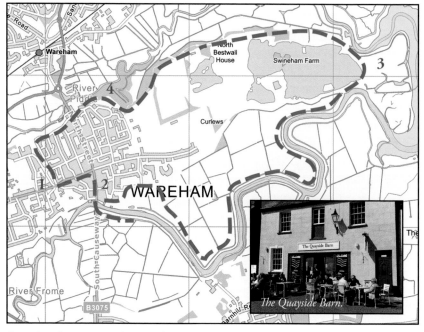

The Quayside Barn.

Start/parking: Stretche Road car park, Wareham SY921873, BH20 4QF.
Terrain: Well signed footpaths, short sections town streets. All level. Parts may be wet/muddy after rain.
Stiles: 1
Public Toilets: Wareham Quay
Maps: Explorer OL15 or Landranger 195

A handsome town with many historic buildings, Wareham is bounded by the rivers Frome and Piddle. This easy, level walk explores the banks of the Frome and the marshland east of Wareham, noted for its birdlife, as well as the town's ancient quay and its Saxon defences.

1. Turn left out of the car park and head into the town centre, signed "Tourist Information". Reaching the Red Lion – one of many fine Georgian buildings erected after fire ravaged the town in 1762 - turn right down South Street. Cross the road at the Black Bear and cross the bridge ahead. Turn left along the bankside path for 200m for further views of the river and priory, 12th century in foundation but largely 16th and 18th century in form. Retrace your steps across the bridge and turn right across the Quay, signed "Two Rivers Walks".

2. ¾ mile: Turn left at the Quayside Barn and right 50m ahead "Two Rivers Walk". Follow the signs left and right behind Lady St Mary Church. Beyond the graveyard, turn right "Two Rivers Walk Swineham Point". Follow the path left, then right behind the caravan park. Continue ahead at the next path junction "Frome Valley Trail River Walk Swineham". The well-beaten path follows the river as it winds its way to Poole Harbour. Look out for wildfowl.

3. 2¾ miles: Bear right "Frome Valley Trail Swineham Wareham" at the path junction. Follow the path around Swineham Point, where a quantity of Roman pottery was found. Walk on past the gravel pit lake. Continue ahead when the path joins a tarred track.

4. 4¼ miles: Reaching the outskirts of Wareham, turn right at the fingerpost and right along the raised bank – part of Wareham's Saxon walls. Continue on the wall walk as it curves west. Follow the lane ahead to North Street. A short diversion left leads to St Martin's, an Anglo-Saxon church with a monument to T.E. Lawrence ("Lawrence of Arabia"), who spent the last years of his eventful life at Bovington Camp. Cross North Street and continue up Shatter's Hill, signed "Walls Walk". The path rejoins the raised bank. Follow it back to the start.

Teashops

Wareham has several teashops and cafés. **The Quayside Barn** (01929 552735) is delightfully situated and en route. It offers teas, coffees, scones, cakes, pastries and a good selection of ice creams, plus ice cream waffles and milk shakes. It has indoor and terrace seating overlooking the quay. Open 10am to late in season, closed Mondays to Thursdays in winter.

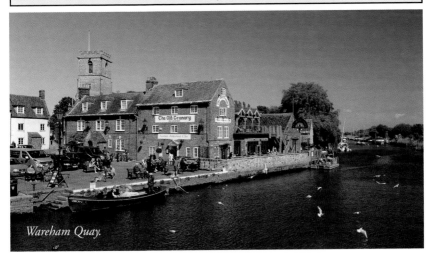

Wareham Quay.

Wareham Walls.

Wareham's Saxon Defences

Wareham provides the best example of Saxon town defences in England. Its earthen ramparts still surround the heart of the town on three sides, whilst the River Frome blocks the south side and the River Piddle provides additional defence to the north. Combining the Two Rivers Walk with the Walls Walk, our route gives a clear picture of Wareham's strategic position, which was well understood by King Alfred the Great, who established Wareham as one of thirty burghs (defended towns) throughout Wessex. A well-developed port, with its easy access to Poole Harbour and the sea beyond, Wareham was a prime target for the seaborne raiders, and suffered the trauma of Viking attack and occupation in 876.

They attacked Wareham again in 998, whilst King Canute's assault in 1015 left the town in ruins. In response, Wareham's defences were strengthened with a stone wall. It is likely some of the stone was used by the Normans to build the then new but now vanished Wareham Castle. Wareham's ancient defences were put to the test during the Civil War when Royalists took the town in 1643. Parliamentarian troops retook Wareham in 1644, forcing their way through the West Gate. In 1940 the outer scarps of the defences were made steeper as a protection against tank attack, providing a remarkably recent example of fortification re-use.

Wimborne - Distance: 4 miles/6.4 km Time: 2 hours Exertion: Easy

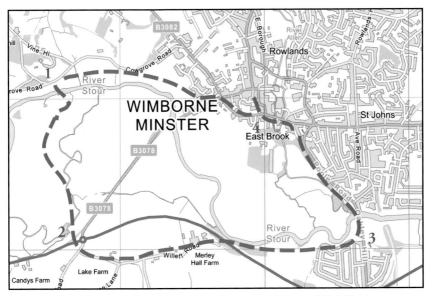

Start/parking: Eye Bridge car park on Cowgrove Road, ST996011, nearest postcode BH21 4EL.

Terrain: Level walking. Footpaths, quiet lanes and town streets. One difficult road crossing.

Stiles: 7

Public Toilets: Wimborne, between Minster and Square.

Maps: Explorer 118 or Landranger 195

Part town and part country, this walk follows attractive footpaths through the meadows and along the banks of the River Stour, as well as exploring Wimborne's historic Square and Minster. Allow extra time for these visits and please take care crossing at Point 2.

1. Cross Eye Bridge. Continue through the kissing gate. Walk ahead, initially keeping the line of trees on your left and then continuing straight ahead (ignoring any side tracks) to a stile. Here, the well-beaten path doglegs slightly left to a gated footbridge. Cross and continue over two stiles to a roundabout.

2. ¾ mile: Cross carefully, signed "Canford Magna Stour Valley Way". Follow the verge for 50m. Recross the main road. Continue ahead on Willett Road. Continue past Lake Farm and Merley Hall Farm into the footpath signed "Wimborne". Follow this under the main road, then fork left through a small gate. Continue on the riverbank path to a playpark. Cross the playpark and

follow the street ahead to Poole Road.

3. 2 miles: Turn left across Canford Bridge, built in 1813 of ashlar Portland stone. Follow Poole Road to a fork. Branch left, and then turn left into Leigh Road. This becomes East Street then King Street. Divert right at the signpost to visit Wimborne's attractive Square and the Minster. Retrace your steps to the King Street signpost.

4. 3 miles: Turn left, signed "Wimborne Model Town". Follow the road as it curves right to a junction. Turn left into Julian's Road and take the first turning right (well before you reach the bridge) up a small lane between houses. At the time of writing, the path ahead crossed rough ground between fencing, but it appears that houses will soon be built here. Beyond the fencing, the path follows the riverbank to Eye Bridge.

The River Stour at sunset.

Wimborne's minster church is a landmark for miles around. Essentially Norman with later additions, the minster is noted for its massive Norman columns. Its history goes back to the 8th century, when Cuthburga, sister of King Ina, founded a nunnery in Wimborne about 705. On the outside of the tower is the early 19th century quarter jack, a British Redcoat dressed in the uniform of the day who strikes his bells with a hammer in each hand. Far older is the astronomical clock inside the tower. Although its case is Elizabethan, its workings are medieval. A stationary Earth is shown at the centre of the clock with the moon and sun revolving around it.

Wimborne Square has a pleasing medley of historic buildings, including the Georgian King's Head Hotel. The Priest's House Museum is next to Tourist Information at 23-27 High Street. A Grade II* historic townhouse, it has ten galleries displaying archaeology, local history and costumes.

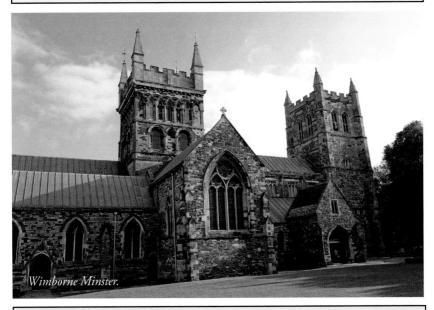

Wimborne Minster.

Teashops

There is a wide choice in Wimborne. **Petit Prince** in East Street (01202 989874) is a family run café, and make their own bread, cakes and vienoiserie on site, specialising in French patisserie. It serves a variety of savouries and a range of teas, coffees and fresh fruit drinks. **Number 9 On The Green** (01202 887765) in Cook Row is a cosy little café with its own bakery. It has an extensive lunch menu and a great selection of home made cakes.

White Mill and Pamphill - Distance: 5½ miles/8.8 km Time: 3 hours
Exertion: Moderate

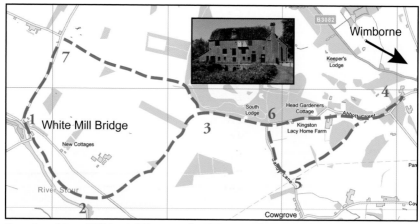

Start/parking: White Mill car park, ST957006, BH21 4BX.
Terrain: Mainly level, quiet footpaths, bridleways and lanes.
Stiles: 9
Public Toilets: None
Maps: Explorer 118 or Landranger 195

Starting from historic White Mill and its handsome nearby bridge, this gentle walk follows footpaths, bridleways and quiet lanes around the edges of Kingston Lacy estate to the café at Pamphill Dairy. The return is equally attractive, with fine views over the verdant countryside.

1. Turn right out of the car park and almost immediately left. Walk past White Mill and continue ahead through a kissing gate. Enjoy a fine view of White Mill Bridge. Follow the riverbank path over a series of stiles as signed.
2. ¾ mile: Turn right as signed. Go through a stile and cross a field to the lane. Turn right and then left after 200m onto a signed bridleway.
3. 1½ miles: Turn right at the crosstracks, signed "Stour Valley Pamphill". After 500m, continue ahead on a lane, past the church to Pamphill Dairy's Parlour Café.
4. 2½ miles: Retrace your steps for 300m and bear left into All Fools Lane as signed.
5. 3¼ miles: Reaching Sandy Lane, turn right as signed "Stour Valley Way".
6. 3¾ miles: When the lane bends right, turn left along the track. Continue ahead "Kingston Lacy Drove" at the first signpost (Point 3). Bear left (west)

at the second signpost. Continue ahead at the third signpost to the lane.
7. 5 miles: Turn left and follow the lane to a T junction. Turn left to the car park.

Teashop
Pamphill Dairy's Parlour Café next door to the farm shop offers cooked breakfasts, cream teas, cakes, light meals and a specials board. It has pleasant indoor and outdoor seating and is decorated with local photographs and rustic paintings. Open all year. 01202 857131.

White Mill Bridge.

White Mill
An 18th century corn mill rebuilt in 1776 on a site marked in the Domesday Book (1086), White Mill retains its original elm and applewood machinery. Unfortunately, this is too fragile to be used, but visitors have a guided tour. Open weekend and Bank Holiday afternoons from Easter to October. National Trust, 01258 858051.

White Mill Bridge
White Mill Bridge is said to be the oldest in Dorset. Its timber pilings have been carbon dated to the 12th century, though what we see today is probably 16th century with later alterations. A metal plaque (1827) warns that anyone wilfully damaging it risks being transported for life. At that time, this meant penal servitude in Australia – a punishment meted out to many involved in the Captain Swing agricultural disturbances of 1830 and to the Tolpuddle Martyrs in 1834.

Child Okeford, Shillingstone and Hambledon Hill - Distance: 5¾ miles/9.2 km (full route) Time: 3 hours (full route) Exertion: Challenging (full route and Loop 2) or Easy (Loop 1)

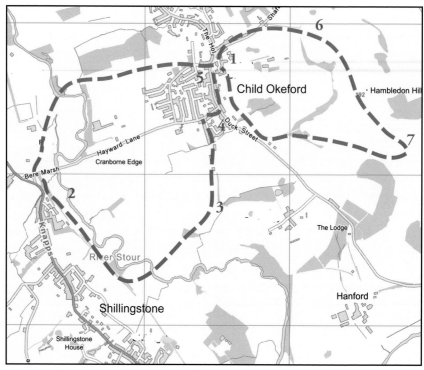

Start/parking: Roadside parking (with care please) by Child Okeford church, ST 835128, DT11 8ED.

Terrain: Footpaths and bridlepaths. One steep ascent and descent on second loop. Parts of first loop liable to flooding after heavy rain.

Stiles: 5

Public Toilets: None

Maps: Explorers 118 and 129 or Landranger 194

This varied and scenic figure of eight walk is made of two loops and thus can be taken as two short walks or one longer ramble. The first loop is an easy, level walk of 3¼ miles from Child Okeford across the water meadows to Shillingstone's attractively restored railway station; the second loop is a shorter, but more demanding, 2¼ mile climb to the summit of Hambledon Hill's Iron Age fort.

Loop One

1. Facing the Baker's Arms, take Hayward's Lane just to the left. After 400m, turn right into a rough track. Turn almost immediately left through a kissing gate as signed. Follow the clear path ahead through small gates and fields to a stream. Divert 40m right to cross by a small bridge. Follow the path ahead to a larger bridge over the Stour. After a third bridge, the path divides. Keep left and cross the field diagonally to a stile. Cross, turn left and follow the short path up to join the railway path. Continue to Shillingstone station.

2. 1½ miles: Continue down the railway path for 700m. Turn left "Child Okeford". Cross the bridge ahead. Continue on the well-beaten path across meadows. Turn left through a metal gate to a track junction.

3. 2½ miles: With the gate at your back, walk ahead (north) and follow the track to a T junction.

4. 3 miles: Do not take the footpath ahead. Turn right to a second T junction. Either turn left and follow High Street to the start to avoid a high stile or cross High Street into the gravelled track ahead (a footpath marked as a Private Drive). Go through a metal kissing gate and bear left through a second kissing gate. Follow the grassy path ahead, keeping the fence on your left. Climb the steps in the churchyard wall and walk through the churchyard. The church is noted for its 16th century greensand tower and 13th century font of Portland stone. Turn left to the Baker's Arms.

Hambledon Hill.

Loop Two

5. 3¼ miles: Facing the pub, turn right. The road divides. Turn right and after 200m divert right into a footpath parallel to the lane. Turn left through the kissing gate. Turn immediately right into an enclosed path. Follow this uphill to a gate. Continue on the steep path to the top of the ramparts. (You might like to pause and imagine the folly of making an uphill assault on the hill fort under a hail of sling stones and spears!)

6. 4 miles: Reaching the summit, follow the ridge path south-east above the impressive ramparts. Exit the fort via a gate and bridleway sign. Continue along the enclosed path to a triangulation pillar.

7. 4½ miles: Turn right through the metal gate and follow the bridleway downhill as signed. Continue beneath the ramparts on the enclosed path to a lane. Turn immediately right over a stone stile into another enclosed path. Reaching a track, either turn left then right up High Street to avoid a high stile, or turn right and almost immediately left through a kissing gate. Follow the grassy path ahead, keeping the fence on your left. Climb the steps in the churchyard wall. Walk through the churchyard. Turn left to the start.

Teashops

Shillingstone Station Café offers hot snacks, rolls, cakes and flapjacks at reasonable prices. Limited opening all year (01258 860696). Alternatively, a half mile diversion along the Manston road from the start leads to **Gold Hill Café**, serving lunches, cakes and a range of teas and coffees (limited opening 07966 599929). **Child Okeford Post Office** (01258 863495) offers morning coffee and afternoon teas, all day breakfasts, light lunches, plus homemade cakes and scones. The Baker's Arms, Child Okeford (at the start) is open daily from 12.

Shillingstone Station.

Sunset on Hambledon Hill.

Hambledon Hill

At 624ft (192m), Hambledon Hill is a superb defensive site with panoramic views. First occupied during the Neolithic period, it was developed in the Iron Age into a formidable hillfort with tiers of ramparts and forms part of a chain of Iron Age hillforts in East Dorset with the Double Dykes on Hengistbury Head at the southern end. In August 1645 Hambledon Hill was the scene of conflict between Clubmen and Parliament's New Model Army (see page 46). Today, it is a peaceful National Nature Reserve, its unimproved lime rich grass supporting many rare wildflowers and butterflies.

Shillingstone Station

Tea in the dining car - a BR Mark I 1950s carriage – is part of stepping back in time to the late steam era at Shillingstone Station and the views over the meadows to Hambledon Hill are a reminder of how wonderful the scenery on the Somerset and Dorset line between Bath and Bournemouth was. There is much to see: the signal box is a rebuild of the original and its lever frames are ready for trains to return, whilst the museum has period photos and railway artefacts; model railways are in the parcel shed. Rolling stock includes a tanker wagon and a gunpowder wagon from a naval base. The 1951 Ruston diesel shunter is being restored, along with an 08 diesel shunter and a Mark III coach.

Compton Abbas - Distance: 3 miles/4.8 km Time: 1½ hours Exertion: Easy

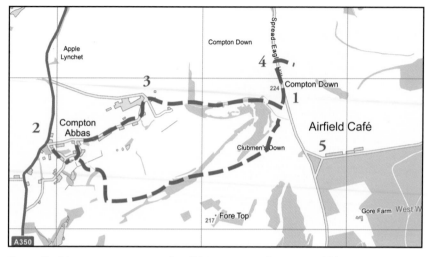

Start: Parking area on west side of B3081 near Compton Abbas at ST 886187.
Terrain: Footpaths and quiet lanes. One moderate ascent and descent.
Stiles: 0
Public Toilets: None
Maps: Explorer 118 or Landranger 183

This stimulating walk over Fontmell Down combines sweeping views with much of natural interest. Cropping by sheep and cattle keeps the turf short, allowing a profusion of plants to thrive, including cowslips, orchids and early gentians. Buzzards, red kites and kestrels quarter the wide skies. Look out too for butterflies - 35 species have been recorded here.

Farmers have grazed their animals on Fontmell Down for millennia, as archaeological analysis from the late Bronze Age dyke – probably built as a stock barrier or defence – has shown. We cross this dyke early on the walk, but this part of the down commemorates not the Bronze Age, but the English Civil War and is known as Clubmen's Down after the Clubmen who assembled here.

Appalled by the damage inflicted by marauding Parliamentarian and Royalist armies, "Clubmen" were formed to defend their territory and property, protect their wives and daughters from rape and themselves from forced military service. Drawn from the local community in several counties, they were particularly strong in Dorset.

Armed with pitchforks, scythe blades and clubs (hence their name), an estimated 2,000 to 4,000 Clubmen confronted Cromwell's New Model Army on Hambledon Hill (please see page 45) in August 1645. One of their most defiant leaders was Thomas Bravell, the Rector of St Mary's, Compton Abbas, who threatened to pistol any man who surrendered.

Although the Clubmen heavily outnumbered the Parliamentarians, they were no match for well-trained, well-armed and battle hardened troops, which included Cromwell's feared cavalry. Attacking from the rear, Cromwell's men easily routed their opponents, killing 60 and wounding many more. Some of the Clubmen made an undignified escape by sliding down the steep slopes of Hambledon Hill on their backsides. Around 400 were captured and locked in Shroton church. After patronising the "poor silly creatures" with a lecture, Cromwell released those who swore to the Covenant as decreed by Parliament.

Rev. Bravell preached in Compton Abbas's 14th century church. Apart from the tower, this later fell into decay and was demolished. Some of the stones from the old church were incorporated in its 1867 replacement, which also includes the re-cut Norman font from its predecessor, three bells and a 1665 chalice.

View from Clubmen's Down.

1. From the parking area go through the gate by the signboard and continue ahead on the footpath over Clubmen's Down. Keep the fence on your left and continue over the Cross Dykes and past a small wood. Walk ahead and downhill as signed by the waymark. Go through a gate and follow the path to the foot of the slope. Turn right through a small metal gate. Keep the field

edge on your left. Pass through another small gate. Follow the enclosed path to a tarmac lane. Turn left, then right at the footpath sign. Walk uphill to the church.

2. 1½ miles: Retrace your steps down the footpath. Turn left onto the tarmac lane and follow it past houses, ignoring side turnings. Reaching a junction, turn right. Follow the lane past the medieval church tower.

3. 2¼ miles: Turn right down the lane "Unsuitable for motors". Keep left when it divides. Continue past a house and follow the grassy track ahead. This climbs steadily uphill to the car park.

4. Walk extension to view Melbury Down. ½ mile: From the car park, follow the grassy path parallel to the road north for 300m to a second parking area. Cross the road carefully to a stile. The views from the path ahead are excellent. Retrace your steps.

5. For the Airfield Café turn right out of the parking area. Take the first turn left and continue for ½ mile.

Teashop
Compton Abbas Airfield Café (01747 811767) has indoor and patio seating, both giving visitors a superb view of aircraft taking off and landing against a backdrop of Melbury Down. Look out too for red kites and buzzards, which have also discovered the rising thermal currents here. The café is open Tuesday to Sunday through the year and provides breakfasts, light lunches and teas, plus a licensed bar. There is a good choice of cooked food, sandwiches, baguettes, teas, coffees and cakes.

An aircraft and red kite at Compton Abbas.